PREPARING FOR
CHRISTIAN
WARFARE

Ten Principles That Will Take Your Faith to the Next Level

GARY PANZER

ISBN 978-1-0980-4406-0 (paperback)
ISBN 978-1-0980-4407-7 (digital)

Christian Faith Publishing, Inc.
832 Park Avenue
Meadville, PA 16335
www.christianfaithpublishing.com

Scriptures taken from the Holy Bible, New International Version®, NIV®. Copyright © 1973, 1978, 1984, 2011 by Biblica, Inc.™ Used by permission of Zondervan. All rights reserved worldwide. www.zondervan.com The "NIV" and "New International Version" are trademarks registered in the United States Patent and Trademark Office by Biblica, Inc.™

Printed in the United States of America

INTRODUCTION

Be transformed by the renewing of your mind.
—Romans 12:2

Before I get started, I need to say this. This is not a book written just for men. It was written for women, teenagers, and everyone who desires to take their Christian faith to the next level in preparation for what lies ahead. In case you haven't noticed, Christianity is at war in America. And we have to prepare ourselves for the spiritual war that is before us. Not only are we at war with the secular world, but we are constantly battling ourselves, our flesh, and our inner demons. If you are a practicing Christian who takes your faith seriously, Satan has painted a target on your back. Maybe things are going well for you now, but you feel you've been stuck in a rut. Or maybe you can't seem to shake the feeling that there has to be more to the Christian life than going to church, paying your tithe, singing hymns, and listening to a sermon every week. Well, you're right. The Christian life is much more than that. I used to say that being a Christian is the hardest thing in life to do. And to a degree, I'm right. It is hard. To not respond to people like we want to respond when they wrong us is hard. I get it. And I could give many more examples, but you understand where I'm going with this. If we want to call ourselves a Christian, then we must take seriously that which Christ calls us to do. And that is to be Christ-like in all situations, to hold ourselves to a higher standard. In his book *Kingdom Man*, Dr. Tony Evans writes, "We should approach the Christian life as a challenge and a quest to conquer." Being a Christian can be as adventurous or mundane as you decide to make it. It all starts with a mindset. And in life, your mind-set is everything. A strong mind-set is the ability to find the positive in a negative situation or circumstance. It will determine how you respond to a crisis and will help you accomplish more than you think you can. The mind controls everything. It has been said that every sin begins with a thought. No action is taken until the thought of said action crosses the mind first. The problem with so many people today is they let their mind control them, instead of them controlling their mind.

There have been a number of studies done among elite military units and athletes to determine what sets them apart from the rest of us. How can they endure so much more pain and punishment to their bodies than we can? What is it about them that when pushed to their ultimate limits, they are able to reach down and find a little more to keep going? The answers all point to the same conclusion. It's simply resilience. When you want something bad enough, you will do everything you can to obtain it. You will let nothing stand in the way of you reaching your goals. The Navy SEALs have a 40 percent rule they live by. In an online article by Forbes.com (2017), Chris Myers writes, "The 40% rule is simple: When your mind is telling you that you're done, that you're exhausted, that you cannot possibly go any further, you're only actually 40% done." He also states, "The human mind is an amazing thing. It both propels us forward and holds us back." Myers closes by saying, "Our ability to deal with challenges, difficulties, and setbacks is defined not by our ability, but rather by our mind-set."

How This Book Came About

My life-group teacher (Sunday school for us, old hats) was planning to be out of town one week and asked me to step in and teach. As I sat at my computer to surf the internet for ideas for a lesson, I decided to delete some emails first and clean out my inbox. Now I get emails from Quora Digest every day. Quora is a site that is open to anyone. It is basically a knowledge site where you can post questions about anything, and usually people with knowledge in that area will respond. The site allows you to choose the categories that are of interest to you so the emails you receive are questions/posts that fall in those categories only. As I was scrolling through, I found this question posed by someone that asked, "How can I obtain the mind-set of a Special Forces Operator?" It was answered by a former Special Operation Forces (SOF) guy, most notably a former Navy SEAL himself. In his answer he gave ten common traits that SEALs all share that give them the mind-set they need to be the best at what they do and get the job done. As I read through, I was captivated by what he said. The thought then came to mind as to how these principles could be applied to our Christian life. So with each principle given, I found some corresponding scripture references and was able to put together a lesson. Afterward, I had several people come up to me and tell me how much they enjoyed the lesson. One person even suggested I put it into a book. This is how this book came about. I've never written a book before, so this is a first for me.

SPECIAL NOTE

When I gave the lesson, I had no intention of using it for a book, so I did not save the article where I could access it again. I copied and pasted to my notes. I tell you this because I have no way of knowing who posed the question on Quora, who answered the question or a date to when it was published. I do not know who to give credit to other than Quora.com. I have searched that site every way I can in hopes that the same article would come up with no luck. Multiple attempts at finding the author of the principles given have failed. I tell you this because I will not take credit for someone else's work. I am currently finishing my degree, and a major push with the university is avoiding plagiarism. I will tell you that the principles given and the examples he uses are not mine. I will note them to Quora. It was not a scholarly article or published anywhere other than that particular website. Although the principles used are not my work, how I've applied them to the Christian life is.

Lastly, the man who gave the principles answered them on how they relate specifically to SEALs. It is safe to say these traits are shared by the Special Operations Forces (SOF) community as a whole, be it Delta Force, Green Berets, or the 75th Ranger Regiment, as well as any SOF units with the Air Force and Marines. I will refer to these groups via SF, Spec Ops, Operators, or Tier One guys. I have learned that the difference between Tier One and Tier Two or Three is more extensive training and the amount of resources that Tier One Operators have available to them that the others don't have. I don't know how many Tier One Teams exist among the SOF, I do know that SEAL Team 6, otherwise known as DEVGRU (Navy Special Warfare Development Group), and the Army's Delta Force (1rst Special Forces Operational Detachment Delta) falls under the Tier

One umbrella, where the other SEAL teams and teams from other branches are considered Tier Two or lower. Regardless of the tier, Special Operations Forces are the tip of the spear, and I'm just glad they're on our side.

This book is written with the focus on the principles given to help you propel your Christian life to the next level. To grow closer to God and to experience Him on a deeper level. I have never served in the military myself, to my deepest regret, but I am proud that my son, Jadyn, is currently serving in the US Army as an MP stationed at Fort Hood, Texas, and my daughter Jordyn wants to be a fighter pilot with the US Navy. She is currently in her senior year of high school. Now let's get started!

A Perfect 10

It's hard to judge the Christian life. How would you? How would you define how good or bad of a Christian someone is? What would we compare it too? "He's a good one because he's in church every week" or "he's not that good because he smokes and drinks beer." How many times have you heard someone say "the people in that church are so judgmental?" After all, isn't that what the Bible says not to do? I heard a pastor years ago use a statistic in his sermon. He said that 86 percent of Americans claimed to be Christian. Well, I would dare say if that were the case, then why do we have all these problems at the level they're at in America today? If 86 percent of Americans who said they were Christians actually took their faith seriously, the problems we do have wouldn't be nearly as momentous as they are today. Abortion would be way down, the divorce rate would plummet, families would remain strong and intact, crime would be down, and so much more. But let's face it. I think a fitting Bible verse here is Titus 1:16, which says "Many claim to know God but deny Him by their actions." People claim to be Christian for a variety of reasons. They were sprinkled (baptized) as a child. They went to church as a child, they believe in God, so that has to count. Oh, and one of my favorites, they don't have to go to church in order to be a Christian. Although I do agree with that last statement, I do have issues with it as well. But this isn't about judging others Christianity. It's about evaluating your own. Oops! Did I strike a nerve? We tend to use the 1–10 scale for a lot of things. We use it to judge someone's pain. On a scale from 1 to 10, with 1 being almost none to 10 being the worst pain you ever felt, how would you rank it? As boys growing up, we would use the 1–10 scale to rank how hot a girl was. Olympic gymnasts and divers are always striving for that perfect 10. It is nothing more than a measurement or a gauge to give context to someone in order to paint a better picture.

So with that said, if I were to ask you, on a scale from 1 to 10, 1 being a brand-new Christian, being born again yesterday, to 10, that having the faith of Abraham, Moses or the apostle Paul, where would you rank yourself? What level would you put yourself? What are you doing to up your level? Are you earnestly growing as a Christian striving to know God better? If not, why not? What's holding you back? When I talk about ranking your faith or leveling up, it sounds like I'm talking about a video game such as Halo or Call of Duty. But this isn't a game. This is serious stuff. Much is at stake. These principles, if put into practice, will indeed take your walk with the Lord to another level, allowing personal and spiritual growth while bringing Him glory in the process.

I

SF Operators All Have a Compelling Why

Any time you talk with a SEAL about how they made it through the grueling training required to get their Trident, they all have a compelling why. Whatever their reason, every elite warrior has a strong why pushing them to succeed at such high levels (Quora).

So let me ask you. Why are you a Christian? What makes you want to be a Christian? I think it's safe to say we're not doing it for the money, and it's surely not going to bring us fame. In some parts of the world, people have been killed for being a Christian. The answer will be different for everyone. As Christians, we all have the same ending point, but vastly different starting points. In 1 Peter 3:15, it tells us to *"always be prepared to give an answer to everyone who asks you to give the reason for the hope that you have."* It's important to know the "why" in order to be more compelling for non-Christians to want to become one. You might be thinking, "Well, that's an easy one. I'm a Christian, so I can go to heaven." If that's the reason you want to be a Christian, then you are well off the mark. I want to go to heaven as well, but that is just a by-product of salvation. Romans 5:1–2 says, *"Therefore, since we have been justified thru faith, we have peace with God thru our Lord Jesus Christ, thru whom we have gained access by faith into this grace in which we now stand. And we rejoice in the hope of the glory of God."* Who doesn't want to live in peace? With all that's going on in the world today, not to mention the inconveniences and tragedies that come our way in life, to know that we can have peace in the midst of those distractions is a very compelling why. But look at the second part of that verse: "*thru whom we have gained access by faith into this grace in which we stand.*" We have access to Almighty God on a daily basis! There is nothing more promising to know that we can come to our Creator at any time for anything. I want to be a Christian because I want to experience Him daily and have that deep personal relationship with Him who sustains me through the perils of life. When I screw up, He picks me up, brushes the dirt off my butt, and says, "It's okay, son, now get back in the game." I want to be a Christian because I want to love the one who loved me first, who loves me regardless of my sins and shortcomings. I want to love Him who not only gave His life for me, but also never gave up on me. Even when I went my own way, He was there. John 15:11 says, "*I have told you this so that my joy may be complete in you and that your joy may be complete.*" Only Jesus can give you meaningful joy. Happiness depends on what happens to you, but if you are in constant fellowship with Him, you can have joy in the worst of circumstances.

Many years ago, I was watching the news, and they were reporting a story on a couple who had six kids ranging in age from three to seventeen. They were all coming back from a family vacation when the van they were in crashed and caught on fire. The parents, who were in the front seats, were able to quickly exit the van, but the crash had damaged the side doors, making them inoperable. The kids were trapped in the van, and the fire spread quickly. They were in a rural area, which contributed to a long response time by the fire department. All six kids perished. A family of eight was cut down to two in a matter of minutes, the living legacy of those parents gone almost instantly. I watched the parents as they gave an interview in front of the cameras. The father was asked what he was feeling after losing his entire family. With a well-composed demeanor, he said that their loss was heaven's gain, and though they didn't understand why this happened, they would continue to draw strength from and trust in the Lord. I saw the same attitude when my younger sister Debbie lost her nineteen-year-old daughter. She died in the early hours of a Saturday morning one week to the day after Debbie got married. A little more than twenty-four hours later, Debbie was in church with hands raised to heaven during the music, worshiping the one true God.

My best friend lost his fourteen-year-old son seven months after my sister lost her daughter. It was on the Fourth of July to be exact. But he never wavered in His faith. In fact, through his pain and suffering, he was able to share the gospel with one of his son's friends, who came over to check on them right after the accident. And because he did, that little boy gave his life to Christ. What do these three examples have in common? Their joy is found in the Lord. Their lives where turned upside down, but they didn't blame God or turn their backs on Him—they worshipped! What a testament as to what Christ can do in your life. This is why I choose to be a Christian.

I couldn't finish this chapter without turning to a man I deeply admire and getting his response as to why he was a Christian. He was my Sunday school teacher for many years and, to my estimation, one of the greatest Bible teachers to ever live. His name is Eric Brand, and you will hear a little more about him later. I asked him why he was a Christian, and here is his answer:

> The meaning of life...who am I, how did I get here, where am I going, what is my purpose? Every man wrestles with is there a God? And if there is, can I know Him? Religion is as old as humanity. From the beginning we have run into "is this all there is...there's got to be more." Solomon addresses this with the Song of Solomon...vanities of vanities, all is vanity." Eric goes on say "Jesus gives me meaning, purpose, value and a reason." Jesus is the answer to life... Heaven is simply a bonus.

My current Bible teacher, Wallace Lock, puts it this way:

> The longer I live the more I know there is a God.
> I know that I will stand before Him. And when
> I stand before Him, it will be better to know
> Him than not. The more I know Him, the more
> I love Him. And it is because I love Him that I
> want to share Him with others. This is why I'm
> a Christian.

I realize it is more important to be a Christian than to know why you are one, but it's important to know why. It gives substance and reason as to why you believe what you believe. It certainly gives it more credibility. Ask anyone in any type of profession, and they will certainly have a compelling why as to what they do. Confidently knowing your why will strengthen your mind-set. It will help you to be bold in your faith. Take some time to evaluate your relationship with the Lord. Think about what He's done for you over the course of your life, how you've seen Him at work in your life and in the lives of others. Then form a compelling why. People will want to know. I want to ready to tell them when they ask.

Takeaways

1. What compels you to want to be a Christian?
2. Would you say being a Christian is more of a title to you or a lifestyle?
3. If you're not a Christian, why not?
4. If you were to be arrested for being a Christian, would there be enough evidence to convict you?
5. Can the people who know you see a love for Jesus in you by your actions and your words?
6. What is the essence of being a Christian?

2

THEY TRAIN THEMSELVES FOR WAR

You rarely meet an overweight Special Forces soldier (Quora). Training for the physical is only one aspect of being prepared for war. I have read a lot of articles and seen a lot of interviews with Spec Ops guys on how they made it through the rigorous training, and they all say the same thing—that making it through training is 80 percent mental and 20 percent physical. Of course, it helps that they are in phenomenal shape when they arrive at selection, and most of these guys were athletes in high school, but the fact remains that they all share that mental component that few of us have, or so we think. You see, we are all capable of pushing ourselves to do more than we think we can, to not give up and never quit; we just don't. So what's the difference between a SF guy and us? The answer is quite simple. It's choice. They have made the choice to continue when their minds are screaming at them to stop, when their bodies are so depleted of energy they feel they can't take another step forward. But they do. They do because they choose to. I know that many things factor in as to why we don't have that mind-set: our upbringing, things we were or weren't exposed to growing up, influences or the lack thereof in our lives. I get it. But the bottom line is that it is nothing more than choice. You would be surprised at what you can do if you choose to.

Training for war is a process. It's where the mind and body come together. As a Christian, how many of you think we are at war? I'm fifty-two years old. I can remember thinking long ago that no matter how bad things got for Christians in the rest of the world, it would never get that bad in America. How naive was I? Granted, it's still not

15

as bad as it is in some countries, but I never dreamed we would be where we are today. And to think this nation was built on Christian principles. Ephesians 6:12 says, *"For our struggle is not against flesh and blood, but against the rulers, against authorities, against the powers of this dark world and against the spiritual forces of evil in the heavenly realms."* In 1 Peter 5:8, it says, *"Your enemy the devil prowls around like a roaring lion looking for someone to devour."* Christianity is at war in America! Abortion on demand, gay marriage, transgenderism, Christian businesses being sued and fined by local governments because they stick to their principles, football teams can't pray on the field after games, the American Civil Liberties Union (ACLU) suing to have one-hundred-year-old crosses placed in public places to honor our fallen soldiers removed, the phrase "Merry Christmas" being taken out of businesses and schools, and the list goes on. At the time of this writing, there is legislation before Congress right now to have "So help me, God" removed from the oath when someone testifies before Congress. This is being spearheaded by Congressman Steve Cohen (D) of Memphis, Tennessee, where I live and work. If you want more proof we are at war, take a look at this information given in the Saturday edition of the *Commercial Appeal* dated April 20 of this year. In an article on *Religion in America Today* it states,

> The percentage of adults who belong to a church plunged by 20 percentage points over the last two decades, hitting a low of 50% last year. Those with no religious affiliation have jumped from 8% to 19%. Catholics dropped from 76% to 63%, while Protestants dropped from 73% to 67%. Hispanics went from 68% to 45%, democrats fell from 71% to 48% and Republicans went from 77% to 69%". The article goes on to say that only 41% of people ages 18-29 go to church, and that thousands of churches in the U.S. are closing every year. (*Commercial Appeal*, 2019, 1)

So how are we training ourselves for war? Psalm 18:13 says, *"You armed me with strength for battle; you humbled my adversaries before me."* There are three components to the word *strength* in this verse. It's physical, mental, and spiritual. Let's look at the physical component first.

Every warrior has above average strength. They have to be well conditioned in order to do their job well. So why is it important for us to be fit as Christians? Well, the body has a way of feeding the mind. When you exercise, endorphins are released in your mind and body. Exercise gives you clarity of thought and improves your focus by allowing more oxygen through the body to the brain. I would think that you would agree that there is no better time for focus and clarity than when we are immersed in God's Word. Not only that, but exercise plays a major part in reducing stress levels.

America the Bountiful

One thing America does not run short on is fast food and all-you-can-eat buffets. And because of this, coupled with a lack of self-discipline, we now hold the title of fattest country in the world. Here in Memphis, we captured the title of fattest city in America in 2012 by Forbes.com. And if that wasn't enough, we also ranked number one in diabetes, high blood pressure, dialysis patients, and sedentary lifestyles. Now that ranking would fluctuate from year to year, but we never drop out of the top 3. The point is that being out of shape can hinder your spiritual life. Being overweight makes you sluggish. It limits your drive, and you don't have that mental sharpness you need when you're reading the Bible. I saw a meme on social media once that said, "I looked out my window this morning and saw two people jogging by my house. It really inspired me to get up and close the blinds." That sure sounds like the America we live in today. Look, this isn't a book on working out and exercise plans and so forth. There are tons of books and literature everywhere you look on that subject, including social media. You need to be able to handle your own body weight, and you need to get your heart rate up for at least thirty minutes. An example would be walking. Start walking at least four days a week at a brisk pace for thirty minutes. See how far you go in that time. Oh, and your phone will tell you. Then each week, try to pick up the pace and cover more ground in the same amount of time. Pretty soon, you will be walking for an hour, then not long after, you will be jogging. As you improve, buy a weighted vest and wear it while you walk. What I suggest is that you set aside one day a week, usually a day you don't have to work. I call it challenge day. Make it tough. Do something challenging for at least one hour. Don't go all out at the start. Just push through until you're done. As you get better, challenge yourself by making it a little harder. What this does is not only improve your health by getting fit, but it disciplines the mind. And that discipline will carry over into consistency with your quiet times with God. By working out and being consistent with it, you are doing much more than getting fit, you are creating a mind-set that is crucial to facing life's challenges. You are setting a foundation for when things get hard in life. When the "unthinkable" happens, you will be able to handle it. You are creating a mind-set that enables you to reach deep inside to overcome any obstacle. For when you get that phone call that says your family member has passed away, or you lose a limb in an accident and now have your life forever altered. It won't faze you like it will others because you have been pushing yourself to go farther than you've gone before to do more than you thought you could. You are preparing yourself for the battlefield of life. You will have done what's hard, so when life gets hard, it's no big deal to you. Get off the couch! Get moving. It's not about how long you live, but the quality of life while you're living. Challenge yourself. You will be glad you did. And you will walk more confidently in your faith.

Now that we covered the physical and mental in the passage above, let's look at the spiritual. This is done with reading His Word, through prayer, fasting, memorizing scripture, discipleship, and mentoring. Let's just briefly touch on these components.

The Word. If we are serious about our faith, then we are reading His Word daily. For those that do, most have a reading plan that they follow. Myself, I have multiple sources like the Daily Bread,

In-Touch.org, or my Daily Devotions for Die-hard Arkansas fans. (They actually publish these for every college team.) But it's not *what* you're reading that matters but *how* you're reading. For most, it probably goes something like this: Read the passage given by the devotional, then read the devotional commentary, pray, and then you're done. It's time to start the day. If you're like me, by the end of the day, you can't remember what you read about hours ago. There is a difference between reading the Bible and studying the Bible. Blowing through several verses and ending quiet time with a quick "please bless me in this area and heal so-and-so and keep my family safe, thank you, amen" is hardly quality time. One way to read the Bible is to let the Bible read you. Are you convicted when you read a certain passage? Is it pointing out something you need to earnestly pray about? Take your time. Soak it in. Even if it's only one verse, dissect it, ponder it, get out a concordance, and look up the root meaning. Look at corresponding verses. Make your quiet time quality time. God speaks to us through His Word. I would hate to miss what He has to say because I hurried through in order to just check a box of things to do today.

Prayer. Like exercise, there have been a lot of books and literature written on prayer. I can't tell you anything new. Are your prayers the same every day? Where are your prayers focused when you pray?

When Food Is Involved, Short Prayers Are Best

I'll never forget the time that I felt a real emptiness when I prayed for some reason. This went on for a period of time, and I had been praying for a couple of weeks that the Lord would begin to pray through me. I prayed that He would turn my prayer life around. Well, He did. After leaving church one Sunday, we had picked up lunch and brought it home. I took my wife's hand and began to bless the food. As I began to pray, I could feel the spirit of God fill my heart. And I prayed like I was on fire. My wife is a godly woman, one of the godliest women you will ever meet. But she was hungry and ready to eat. And while she sat there in silence, whittling away from starvation, I was lost in prayer and praise. By the time I was done, the food was cold, and I thought I was going to have to revive my wife with CPR.

Look, the bottom line is this: Are our prayers focused on what God can do for us? Or is the focus on Him and His will? My Bible teacher, Wallace, whom I mentioned earlier, said it this way, "God invites us to pray *with* Him, not just *to* Him." I had never thought of it that way. If someone said, "I'd like to pray with you," you would probably feel honored by that. That is what God is saying when he invites us to pray. He wants to pray with us. Are we the ones doing all the talking during prayer? Or do we listen for Him? God will speak to you through prayer if you will be silent and let Him. Whatever you do, open your prayers with praise. He knows what you need and what you're going to ask for before you ask. So open and close your prayers with praise. This is exactly what Jesus did when he taught us to pray what we call the *Lord's Prayer* found in Matthew 6:9–13. He opens and closes with praise.

Do you pray the Word of God? Our former pastor, Dr. Adrian Rogers, used to say the prayer that gets to heaven is the prayer that starts in heaven. Pray His Word over your family, this country, and our leaders. Isaiah 55:11 says, "*So is my word that goes out from my mouth: It will not return to me empty, but will accomplish what I desire and achieve the purpose for which I sent it.*" Pray like it matters, because it does. Our country, our future, our families, and deepening our personal relationship with the Father are at stake. I will share with you one thing I do when I pray that you may find beneficial. Many times when I pray, I pray while listening to music. You can go to YouTube and type in "Epic Music." It is compiled with movie scores, music so motivating that I begin to pray with so much passion. It literally feels like my prayers are being rocketed to heaven. When I do this, I pray for things that otherwise wouldn't have come across my mind. To me, this is awesome. Whether it's epic music, or worship music, you will find this a moving experience. And I can't help but thinks that it brings a smile to God's face. If you want to give it a try, go here: https://www.youtube.com/watch?v=E-X1gvLCOHM&list=PLoM9CL4f9khd3a38h6Wk0bh-jPzj0svcRH&index=15&t=1925s Start at the 25:20 mark.

Fasting. This gets preached on from time to time, but I have rarely heard much emphasis placed on fasting. Fasting is denying yourself so that we can better focus on God and His will. I've done this a few times myself, once for three days. And I will say that during that time, my focus was so on God that I didn't get hungry once. He truly sustained me. Every time I would start to get hungry or think about food, I started to pray. And that is really what fasting is all about, our focus on Him. Eric Brand taught it this way: "If I got four friends and played the Memphis Grizzlies (an NBA team) in a basketball game, we would get whipped 200–0. But then we practiced two nights a week and played them again, we might only lose by 175 points. So we practice four nights a week, and only lose by 145 points and maybe even score five points ourselves."

The point is, fasting is just practice. Let's say you cut out coffee for a week, but on Thursday you give in and have a cup. Then you say, "Gary, I screwed up and had a cup of coffee. I failed." You didn't fail. Why? 'Cause it was just practice. When you fast, your focus is pinpointed on the Lord. You're denying yourself of something you enjoy in order to hear from Him. And it's good practice. So when something happens or temptation to do wrong arises, you are zeroed in on God and are better equipped to handle it or flee, depending on the circumstance.

Memorizing Scripture. When a warrior is in battle and things go wrong, he reverts back to his training. At Basic Underwater Demolition / SEAL School (BUDs), during the water competency phase, the instructors will take the SEAL wannabes to the bottom of the pool, breathing from air tanks while blindfolded. The instructors then create havoc by shutting off their air, kinking hoses/airlines, and watching them work the problem. It's all a part of going with what they know and what they've been taught.

What do you revert to when bad thoughts and temptations coming knocking on your mind's door? Memorizing scripture is an ideal way for you to combat those thoughts and temptations when they come your way. When Satan tempted Jesus in the desert, Jesus reverted back to and quoted scripture. He didn't argue, discuss, or even converse with Satan. The Word was enough. And when we start to get anxious or scared in a crisis, temptation or a difficult situation, we can speak the Word of God and the one who comes to attack us will turn and run with his tail between his legs. He has to! Hebrews 4:12 says, "*The Word of God is alive and powerful, sharper than a double edge sword.*" The written Word carries a lot of weight. When the devil is whispering in our ear, if we have God's Word engrained in our hearts and minds, then we have the weapon we need for success. Remember, we are in a war. Trying to fight this battle without His Word is like a soldier running into battle without a gun. Memorize key scriptures that will help you navigate through life and you will walk more boldly and confidently in your faith making you a much stronger Christian. I guarantee it!

Discipleship. I wasn't discipled growing up. And it hurt. Oh sure, I went to church, Sunday school, and I was taught right from wrong. But I wasn't taught how to biblically deal with adversity, be a husband, deal with people of differing views, and all sorts of issues that we face in our daily lives. Discipleship is just learning how to be more like Christ. How would Jesus respond in this situation? Just like the bracelets would say "WWJD," what would Jesus do? And that's the goal, right? To be more and more like Christ. That's what discipleship is, and it is a very important aspect of taking your faith to the next level. It can be formal or informal, but if you haven't been discipled, find someone who would be willing to take you under their wing. You will certainly grow in your walk with the Lord.

Mentoring. Everyone needs a mentor, regardless of age. If you've been through discipleship, it's time to turn around and disciple someone. Pass down what you know. All your life experiences can be vital in the growth and development of others. If your kids are grown and out of the house, be a big brother or a big sister to someone. Get involved with the youth department in your church. Lead a Girl or Boy Scout troop. There are lots of ways you can be a mentor to someone who needs it.

The Magnificent 7

At my house, we always had an open-door policy. We were the go-to house for friends of both my kids. They would always come over, and when they did, they didn't knock. They just came in. My wife and I preferred it that way. They knew they always had a place to come to where they were always welcome. They were like our other sons and daughters. My son, Jadyn, was really close to six other boys all through high school. So at the beginning of his senior year, I would send each one of those seven boys a group devotional text about midweek. I did this every week for the entire school year. Things they could relate to, coupled with the Word of God. In early May, when they were all about to graduate, I had them come over one night for steaks and the last devotion, to be done together in person. No T-shirts or flip-flops were to be worn. They had to wear a collared shirt and look presentable. After dinner, my wife, Kristin, and I took them to the living room, and then one at a time, they told us about their last year in school and what they took away from the devotional texts. After each took their turn, I then gave the last devotion and afterward, had them come up one at a time and presented each with a challenge coin that had the whole armor of God stamped on it. Kristin and I would then tell them what each of them meant to us. Afterward, we circled around the coffee table, arm in arm, and I prayed Colossians 1:9–14 over them. When it was over, we all went outside and smoked cigars, wife included.

Ever since our kids were little, after supper every night, we would have a short devotion. And with two kids that both have ADD, it had to be short. Even as they got older, through the eye rolling and mumbling from time to time, we devoted! (New word I made up.) Quite often, my kids' friends would come over for dinner, and then afterward, we would devote. It was cool to hear this young girl, my son's friend, tell us that she really enjoyed that and wish they did that at her house. You never know the impact you may have on someone doing something as simple as that. And when your kids have their own families one day, it's likely they will do the same with them.

Do you want to know what it takes to be a mentor? Be willing. All it cost me was ten minutes a week in time and the cost of nine steaks and coins, a small price to pay for the opportunity to invest in the lives of seven special young men. I will always remember and cherish that night. Invest time in someone and help take their faith to the next level. Reading the Bible, prayer, fasting, scripture memorization, discipleship, mentorship—these are the resources we have to grow closer to God and taking our faith to the next level. Use them and exhaust them to become the man or woman that God has destined you to be.

Takeaways

1. How are you taking care of yourself physically?
2. What can you do to physically challenge yourself weekly or biweekly?
3. Are you consistent with reading God's Word every day? If not, find a Bible plan to follow.
4. Are you setting aside time each day to pray? Are you praying with your spouse? Make this a priority!
5. Are you in a disciple group? Are you disciplining your children?
6. Do you have a mentor? If not, get one!
7. Can you think of someone to mentor? Coworker, neighbor?
8. Set aside one day a month for fasting. Make it the same day of every month. Twelve or twenty-four hours.
9. Are you memorizing scripture? Try and make it a goal to memorize at least one verse a week.

3

SF Guys Wake Up Early, They Set Goals

The author of these principles said that he had yet to meet a SEAL, active or retired, who doesn't wake up early (Quora). Again, that could probably be said of all the SOF guys. After all, these warriors have been getting up early since boot camp, and probably before. I have read many articles by successful businessmen, CEOs, and athletes that claim part of their success is a routine of getting up early, exercising, and getting their day started while the rest of the world slept. There is something fulfilling when you are up before the sun and getting an early start to the day. It gives you a feeling of accomplishment. For Spec Ops guys, they wake up early and pursue their goals with relentless focus (Quora). And that's really what this chapter is about—your goals.

Let me ask you this: What are your goals as a Christian? Do you have any goals? Most Christians will live their lives without much accomplishment because they don't think of their spiritual life as something to set goals for. But Proverbs 21:5 says, "*The plans of the diligent lead to profit.*" How do we "profit" in our Christian life? When we set goals for ourselves and meet those goals, it propels our faith to the next level. And what does the "next level" mean? We see characteristics of God that maybe we haven't experienced before. An example would be that you or a loved one has cancer. We know God to be the Great Physician but can't personally experience that characteristic until He intervenes and heals us. When we set goals for our Christian lives, God sees that we are taking our walk with Him seriously and shows us more of Him. Now this isn't a guarantee that He will heal the cancer, but we still get to experience a part of God during that time of sickness that we may not have gotten to experience otherwise.

It could be a small goal, like reading through the Bible in a year. If you've never done that, start there. There are any numbers of things that you can do, and when you meet that goal, then set another one. Set a goal with a family member or a friend so that you can both pursue it together. You are being intentional with your faith when you set goals. And wisely setting goals leads to better results. Proverbs 16:9 says, "*In his heart a man plans his course, but the LORD determines his steps.*" In other words, we have our ideas and make our plans, but God will ultimately accomplish His sovereign desires. Do our goals make room for the unexpected? If in pursuing a goal, God gives you a different direction, we are to be obedient and change course, setting that goal aside for now. Maybe you come back to it later or maybe not. But His direction in pursuit of goals is always best.

My Everest

My coworker and good friend Forrest is an avid hiker, but not your average hiker. This guy goes out west to the Rockies every year and hikes up a 14,000 foot plus mountain (14er). He has summited several in Colorado and Montana. These aren't technical hikes that require climbing equipment, but you have to be in great shape in order to be successful. Loving the western outdoors myself, I accepted his invitation to join him. Another firefighter was supposed to join us but backed out, so Forrest brought his stepdaughter Desiree and her friend Amber, both in their mid-twenties and both first-time hikers to this extent, like me. I knew this was going to be hard, and summiting this mountain was my goal! I was prepared for it mentally, or so I thought. Although I had three months of CrossFit under my belt, I was still not in the shape I needed to be in. But I love Colorado, so I went. The morning of the hike, we got up early and packed for the hike, although we got a later start than we wanted. Forrest said we should be off the mountain and back at camp by two o'clock that afternoon, so we left everything at camp with the exception of food and water. At the put in, we walked a gravel road that took us into the woods and to the trail that would lead up the mountain. Unbeknownst to Forrest, as the road curved ninety degrees to the right, the trailhead would branch off left. We didn't see the sign and continued right. A mile and half down the road, Forrest realized his mistake, and we doubled back. So three miles into the hike, just to get to the trailhead now put us more behind. But the scenery was gorgeous so I didn't mind the detour. The hike was toughest for me, but I lagged on. Once above the tree line, it got to the point that in order for me to continue, I would take ten steps and rest for twenty seconds. My legs were blasted, and I had quit a thousand times in my mind. But something kept pushing, and her name was Amber. I kept telling myself to keep going, step by step. I thought of the Lone Survivor, Marcus Luttrell, and what he went through. But every so often, I considered my journey done. And Amber would just say, "No, you're not." She would say, "We're a team, and we are going to do this together." She would tell me, "You didn't come all the way out here just to quit." And sometimes when I had to stop and have a mini stroke, she just stopped on the trail with me but didn't say a word. When I moved, she would move. She was just so patient. Without her encouragement, I wouldn't have made it. Thank you, Amber!

The Summit—Almost

So we think we are nearing the top. Hikers before us that summited would pass us on the trail on their way down and tell us, "Just a little farther. There is where you want to be." Once we cleared the top, my biggest fears came true. It was a false summit. We still had more to go. At one point, the trail disappeared and it was just rocks. Finding the most stable rock to step on was time consuming. Nothing frightening, just hard. This slowed us down a bit because more effort was needed to climb these boulders. And my legs were already like jelly. We got to within two hundred feet of the summit and stopped to rest. Forrest said it would only take thirty minutes to make it to the top and back to where we were. But he didn't take into account my already shot legs. And then I noted the time: 3:30 p.m. Why does that matter? We were supposed to be back at camp at two o'clock. We were still near the summit and hadn't started down yet. It was, at minimum, two to three hours back down the mountain and to the car, and we still had to hike through the woods. It gets darker faster there because the sun will dip behind the mountains. Combine that with the canopy of the forest blocking sunlight and the fact that all our gear, lights, food, and water was at camp, and you can see why I was becoming scared. I told Forrest if he wanted to summit, then I would wait right there for him until he got back. I knew it would take me another forty-five minutes to get to the top with the condition of my legs and then another forty-five to get back to where we currently were. Forrest had failed to take into account our skill level. The girls agreed that we needed to turn back. We were now in a race with the sun. Forrest agreed but said that we were only fifty feet from the 14,000-foot mark and he wanted us to make the 14ers club. I sprinted there with all I had. We took pictures and high-fived each other before descending. When we finally made it back to the car, it was dark. You don't want to be stuck in the Rocky Mountain Wilderness at night with no light or supplies. If we had gotten stuck on the mountain, we wouldn't have died or anything. Just been real cold, hungry, and cranky. The sun would have risen the next day, and we could have walked on out. We were 200 feet short. Did we miss anything? Not really. The view doesn't change much in 200 feet. Did we hit our goal? No. Funny thing is, I told myself all the way going down the mountain that I would never do this again. What's the point? What's the purpose? This was stupid. And on and on. But on the flight home, I couldn't help but think what an awesome experience this was. I was finally tested, physically and mentally, and for all intents and purposes, I passed. I had help, but I passed. Forrest and I are already planning to go back the summer of 2020.

The whole purpose of that story is this: it's good to set goals, but it's not whether we make it or not. It's the journey that's going to bring you the experience. The journey will be what's going to make fond memories. And it's the journey that is going to bring you closer to the Lord. And that is what the Christian life is all about—going on a journey with God. Think about what you would like to do, then set goals. Strive for them. Just make sure you let Him lead you along the way. Setting goals will help take your faith to the next level.

One of your goals should be to get to the point in your Christian walk that you have no faith at all. What do I mean by this? When I first became a Christian, I certainly trusted the Lord by faith. And the more my faith grew, the more certain I was God was real and was personally interacting in my life. As I would pray about specific things throughout the years, I could look back and see how the Lord intervened through those prayers. How He answered my prayers either on my behalf or on behalf of whoever I was praying for. I can turn and look back at the past and see how He worked in my life to bring me to where I currently am. The more He answered, the stronger my faith grew. And now after years of walking with Him and witnessing what He has done in my life and the lives of others, I have no more faith at all. Faith is believing in the unseen. I've seen enough over the course of years that my faith has simply turned to knowing. I know He is there. I know He will answer my prayers; whether or not it's the answer I want, He will answer. I know that He is constantly at work in my life and the lives of others. I know He loves me and wants the best for me. I know that He is alive and well. I know my salvation is secure. Sure, this is merely a play on words. To me, my faith is to the point that I know I can depend on Him in all things. I know God is in control, and He knows what's best. Eric Brand taught this lesson years ago, and it has stuck with me ever since.

Takeaways

1. What are some goals you have already accomplished in life?
2. What would you like to accomplish in your Christian life?
3. Is anything standing in your way of accomplishing those goals?

4

THEY HAVE A DEFINITE PURPOSE

All Special Forces Operators have a definite purpose to complete the next mission and bring their team home safely. All of them have a definite purpose pushing them forward and keeping them on their toes (Quora).

As a Christian, what is your purpose? Have you found your purpose? We all share some common purpose such as glorifying God through worship, sharing His gospel, serving outside of our church, serving our family, but what is your specific purpose? It's going to be different for all of us, and God has a specific purpose for us all.

Ephesians 2:10 says, *"For we are His workmanship, created in Christ Jesus for good works, which God prepared beforehand, that we should walk in them."*

The purpose God has for us is not always an easy find. I'm still wondering and praying about my purpose. Some people discover their purpose by accident. Your purpose should be something that you have a passion for. Many times God will bring you through a specific crisis or event in order to show what your purpose is. I mentioned my sister losing her daughter in an earlier chapter. Because of that, she now works for a funeral home assisting and ministering to others who has lost loved ones as well. And she absolutely loves it! She knows that is what God wants her to do. A man in my Sunday school class named James Lindsey is another perfect example. James served in the Marine Corps as a machine gunner for six years. One day, he was called in to a meeting thinking he was being promoted. Instead, they informed him that he was one of twenty-four marines in the nation that was chosen to the honor guard that would go over and represent the United States for the Queen of England's Silver Jubilee. After leaving the Corps, he later joined an all-volunteer group called the Marine Corps League in 2008. This group would provide honors for veterans' funerals. He loved serving in that capacity. In August of 2016, he became the director of West Tennessee State Veterans Cemetery here in Memphis. Like my sister, he uses his position to minister to the families of our nations heroes. He has stated that this is his purpose, and he is so grateful for it. Your purpose can be anything, but what is so important is that you use it for God's glory and to expand His kingdom!

Don't get the idea that in order to have a purpose, you can't get paid for it. Some people say that if you get paid, then it's not considered a ministry. I disagree. On the fire department, as a paramedic, I would witness to everyone who got into my ambulance. Yes, I was on duty and getting paid, but not for witnessing. I used my position to glorify the King and expand His kingdom. I used my job as a ministry to the lost. After all, I got saved while riding an ambulance, so I thought maybe other people can get saved riding an ambulance as well.

Welcome to Bellevue, Dr. Gaines

In order to fulfill your purpose, you need to have a vision. I go to a big church. Some would call it a megachurch. But whatever. When I started going there, Adrian Rogers was the pastor. If you've never heard Dr. Rogers, pull him up on YouTube. He had a thundering voice and could command any type of audience. Throughout his career, he met with US presidents and other people of high stature. He was once asked to preach at the National Cathedral and was the president of the Southern Baptist Convention multiple times. And oh, how he loved the Lord. He preached with intellect and humor and had a unique way of making it relatable to everyone. Under his leadership, the church grew tremendously. We were encouraged to go out into the world and make a difference. The thing is, though, no one from the outside could use the church if it wasn't church related.

If it wasn't sponsored by the church, the church couldn't be used. Dr. Rogers retired in 2005, then died later that year.

It wasn't too long after his retirement that a new pastor was chosen, Dr. Steve Gaines from Gardendale, Alabama. With new leadership came a new vision. He opened up the church to be used by outside groups. Every year, the school system has their in-service training at Bellevue, and the church feeds them all. About seven thousand people. We supply materials for the teachers to take back to the classrooms. We now let almost all the local schools use the church for graduation ceremonies. We purchased a dental van that is staffed with dentists and aides and go into the projects of Memphis and offer free dental care. With the addition of the new minister of music, Vacation Bible School now houses four thousand to five thousand kids for a week every summer. Under the leadership of Brother Steve, we now host Bellevue Loves Memphis workdays every quarter that encompasses anywhere from eight hundred to two thousand people that will go out in groups across the city and work on projects for schools, other churches, nursing homes, block parties, and whatever else needs done. And it's totally free to the people it's being done for. Bellevue Loves Memphis has gotten so big that requests come from all over and are put on a waiting list. There is so much going on with and in the church that didn't used to, that I don't have room in this book to list it all. But I can say that although the overall purpose of bringing people to Jesus didn't change, the way we go about doing it has. And it's remarkable.

Maybe you get paid for your purpose, and maybe you don't. That's not important. It could be volunteering to visit prisons on weekends or participating in a special needs class. Whatever it is, though, keep in mind two things. Your purpose can change in an instant. God has the ultimate authority to redirect what He wants you to do at any time. Secondly, don't get so involved that you start to neglect your family, yourself, or other responsibilities. I've done this before. I got so caught up in doing for God that I started missing out on God. Being busy is not the goal here. It's not up to you to do everything. Sometimes you just have to say no if it looks like you're overextending yourself.

There is nothing more gratifying then fulfilling your purpose in life. Too many people don't. Don't be one of those people. God has a calling for you. Seek His face as to what your purpose is. Pray, fast, and stay in His Word. Ask others to pray on your behalf. Find your purpose and then watch your faith grow.

Takeaways

1. What purpose or passion has God called you to do?
2. Are you pursuing that purpose? If not, why not? What is holding you back?
3. If you're unsure, are you praying and fasting to hear from God on your purpose?
4. How committed are you in pursuing your purpose?

5

OPERATORS CULTIVATE STRONG BONDS WITH THEIR TEAMMATES

SEALs don't actually refer to themselves as SEALs. They refer to them-selves as "Team Guys." And with good reason. In BUD/s, recruits are taught that they are only as strong as the man next to them. You will never meet a group of men who share a stronger bond than elite warriors and Special Forces soldiers. SEALs know the importance of team work and camaraderie, and they cultivate a strong team culture and sense of family in everything that they do (Quora).

There are other professions that share the teammate mentality. Firefighters and police officers are another example of team guys. Being a firefighter myself, I can walk into any fire station in the coun-try, and maybe the world, and be welcomed with open arms. It's part of the profession. It's part of knowing that we have been through the same training, stresses, and dangers that our profession requires of us. It's knowing that not everyone is cut out to do the things that we do that forges that bond. It is truly a brotherhood, and it's the best thing about being a firefighter or police officer. I love the way that firefight-ers and police look out for each other. I have been pulled over a few times by the police, and as soon as they realize I'm a firefighter, they let me go. I have never gotten a ticket in twenty-three years.

As proud as I am to be a firefighter, I am even more proud to be a Christian. Not just a Christian, but a true Christ follower. One who takes their faith seriously and has surrounded myself with other godly men. This has been a challenge for me as the fire service is not conducive to a Christian lifestyle. More often than not, I will see guys sit down at the table, bow their head, bless their food, and then drop all kinds of F-bombs in their next sentence. Don't get me wrong, I have met some truly godly men on the job, but they are the exception rather than the norm. If you're reading this book, then most likely you are part of the greatest brotherhood or sisterhood of all. You are part of the family of God! A child of the One True King! It doesn't get any better than that. And within that broad brotherhood / sisterhood, there should be a few select people in your inner circle. You need people who can relate to you, your personality, and who will hold you accountable. You should set aside time to interact with those people outside of church. Get close to them and to their families. Proverbs 27:17 says, *"As Iron Sharpens Iron, so one person sharpens another."* I understand that the demands of a family, work, church, and kids' events can stretch you pretty thin. But it is imperative to your growth that you have a few people who you know you can count on, who are praying for you at all times, and who can turn to you and you to them when needed. You have to put effort into these kinds of relationships. That war we talked about should not be fought alone. We are actually fighting two wars: the war with the liberal / secular / socialist / progressive movement for the soul of our nation and a daily war where you are constantly battling self. You can't do it alone, nor should you try. We need each other.

Every Sunday morning before life group, a small group of men, about four or five, will go out in the hall and pray over our teacher Wallace. As my fire department schedule keeps me away from church for three Sundays in a row, Wallace and I make it a point to talk at least once a week by phone. We know we can count on each other.

Establishing Bonds

As I mentioned before, tight relationships are a result of being intentional. Find something that you can do with other men or women. My wife, Kristin, really felt led by the Lord to host a bunch of women from our life group class over for a woman's group. Her first meeting, twenty-five women showed up. At the same time, the

35

guys met at the house of one of the men in our class for a Bible study and some fellowship. Bonds are being forged here. Every month we have dinner with the same couple. One month is at our house, the next, their house. We've been doing this for over a year. We rarely see each other any other time, so we are intentional about keeping this relationship going. They are a fascinating couple whom I love to death and would do anything for. This is being intentional in our relationship.

One of the best times I've had was when I did a Tough Mudder with my best friend Rick, my son Jadyn, and his friend Cameron. If you don't know what that is, look it up on YouTube. It's a ten- to twelve-mile obstacle course with twenty obstacles to overcome. But here's the deal, the course is made so that you can't do it by yourself. You will need help negotiating the obstacles. It takes about four hours to complete. It was so cool to see hundreds of people of all different backgrounds come together to run this race. Strangers, pushing you up an obstacle and you turning around to pull others up. Athletes, office workers, salespeople, factory workers, college kids, democrats, republicans, hippies, Christians, and I'm sure an atheist or two, along with people of all different races, putting differences and beliefs aside for one common goal. And it wasn't easy. Do you want to tighten a bond with a few men or women? Get together and do a Tough Mudder or a Spartan race. You will have a great time and have an experience to remember. I guarantee it. You don't have to do something as physical as a Tough Mudder. Go bowling, drive go-carts, go to the shooting range, go fishing. The list of things you can do is endless. Just meet regularly. Don't wait for someone to call and ask you. You may be waiting a while. You make the call. You make the plans. It will pay off. And as long as you're being intentional, your faith level has nowhere to go but up.

Takeaways

1. Do you have people you are close to that you share common interest with?
2. Do you interact with them on a regular basis?
3. Do they keep you accountable by asking you hard personal questions?
4. What are you doing to forge bonds with other like-minded Christians?
5. Make it a point to talk to someone close at least once every week.

6

They Take Extreme Responsibility and Ownership

You will never hear a good operator offset the blame to someone else. No matter what has happened, every SF guy takes extreme ownership and responsibility for their lives. They don't blame others for their failures, and they don't let themselves off the hook. The buck stops with them (Quora).

Genesis 3:6 is what I believe is the most tragic verse in the Bible: *"When the woman saw that the fruit of the tree was good for food and pleasing to the eye, and also desirable for gaining wisdom, she took some and ate it. She also gave some to her husband, WHO WAS WITH HER, and he ate it."*

This is the one chapter that specifically addresses men, although there is something to be learned by women as well. The first sin in the Bible is not Eve eating the forbidden fruit. The first sin is Adam standing idly by and doing nothing about it. It is Adam's failure of leadership when it was needed most. In his book *Kingdom Man* (*KM*), Tony Evans says that Adam willingly relinquished his God given right to leadership. Our country is suffering today because of a lack of leadership by men. About 76 percent of black communities have no father in the home. Teen suicide, teen pregnancy, drug use, juvenile crime, and on and on are prevalent because the dad is absent, or if present, is so caught up in other things rather than paying attention to what's going on in the lives of his family.

38

When men blame others or keep silent like Adam did, they give up their opportunity to approach the Christian life as a challenge and a quest to conquer and have instead settled to live as responders (*KM*). Responders only respond after an incident has occurred. Wouldn't it be much better to mitigate issues before they turn into problems? This can't be done when the man fails to take ownership and be responsible for those under his care. So let me ask you men, are you stepping up and being the leader in your home that God has ordained you to be? How long do you wait to clean out the garage after your wife asks you to? What about the leaky kitchen sink that she's been asking you to fix and even went so far as to buy the replacement kit that has been sitting in the box tucked away in the bedroom for six months? Let me be clear, saying you will take care of it is not taking care of it. This requires action on your part. Take ownership, take responsibility. Lead your family well and always be involved in the lives of your kids. Because the kind of leader you are to your family will most likely be the kind of leaders your kids will be to theirs. I don't have any biblical passage to back this up, but I have always felt that when we stand before God we will be judged most harshly on three things: what we did with Jesus in this life, what kind of husband/wife we were to our spouse, and what kind of father or mother we were to our kids. Our families are our first priority, our ministry. For you dads, I have heard it taught that the way your kids see you is how they see God. If you don't raise your kids, the world will. And the responsibility for how that turns out will fall on you. You must lead by example. Does your family see you pray? Do you pray with them outside of meals? Do they see you praise? Are you teaching them the Bible? How do they see you treat your spouse? I could go on but you get the point.

Boot Camp

Long ago, there was a talk show on television called the *Jenny Jones Show*. It was one of many talk shows at the time, and one day while the kids were at school and the wife at work, I stumbled on it while channel surfing. I stopped there because what captured my attention was this hulk of a drill sergeant screaming at this kid, putting the fear of God into him. The show that day was what to do when your kid gets out of hand. They had parents bring their bratty punk kids who were disrespectful and disobedient onto the show. What the kids didn't know was that this drill sergeant was waiting to come out and confront them. What made it even better was the fact that the parents had given this drill sergeant permission to take them away for a couple of days for some reforming. And the cameras followed. He broke their spirit and set them straight so when they reunited with their parents, they were much better behaved.

In watching this, I thought what a great idea to have something like this here in Memphis: a boot camp for troubled youth. So I called a sheriff's deputy, who I had seen was running for mayor, and spoke with him about the idea. We met for lunch, and he loved the idea. So we met again, only this time he brought a lawyer. After that meeting came another with even more people involved. Every time we met, more people in certain professions that we would need to make this happen were there. It got to the point that we were even looking at properties where we could have this boot camp. It was really exciting, and I prayed fervently for it to happen, believing this is what God was wanting me to do. But then it stopped. I would call the lawyer and leave messages, to no avail. No returned calls for over a month. Finally I was able to get through to him, and he told me that they could no longer pursue this at that time. He really didn't give a reason other than they had other priorities. One night at the station, I was out on the back patio praying aloud to God, asking what went wrong. "Why did all this come to a halt when it looked like it was going to take off?" And right there He answered me. I had a reality check from God. He simply said, "Gary, how can I expect you to lead these troubled kids and a staff responsibly when you're not being the leader you need to be in your own home?" Wow! All I could say was, "I hear you, Lord, loud and clear."

And at that moment I was at peace with this boot camp not happening. And because of that, I turned my focus to where it should've been all along—being a better leader to my family. That experience was humbling, and it helped me refocus on what was more important. I took ownership of that, and it made me a better man.

Maybe you're divorced and don't get to see your kids all the time. Do not let that stop you from being the mom or dad your kids need. Do not let your past mistakes dictate what kind of a parent you can be and ought to be. Don't let those mistakes inhibit you from being the husband or wife you are called to be. Use them for the greater good. Use them to grow you, build you, and catapult you to greatness. Take ownership of your responsibilities and walk boldly and confidently knowing that when it comes to your family, your job, your walk with Lord, failure is *not* an option.

Ezekiel 22:30 says, "*I searched for a man among them who would build up the wall and stand in the gap before me for the land, so that I would not destroy it; but I found no one.*" Be that man, that woman, that family who stands in the gap for the Lord. So much depends on it.

Now let me quickly contrast that verse with Job 1:6–8: "*One day the angels came to present themselves before the Lord, and Satan also came with them. The Lord said to Satan, "Where have you come from?" Satan answered the Lord, "From roaming through the earth and going back and forth in it." Then the Lord said to Satan, "Have you considered my servant Job? There is no one on earth like him; he is blameless and upright, a man who fears God and shuns evil."*

There is one thing that stands out to me in this passage. Satan didn't ask God for permission to attack Job; rather, God offered Job up to Satan. Think about that. God had so much confidence in Job that He offered him to Satan. So let me ask you this: if a conversation where to take place between God and Satan today, would your name come up? Would God have enough confidence in you because of the way you take ownership of your faith, your family, and your integrity to offer you up to Satan confidently knowing you would pass the test? Your life is yours and no one else's. It's your journey. Own it.

Takeaways

1. Is there anything that you haven't taken ownership or responsibility for that you need to?
2. Are you holding your kids accountable and making sure they know what that means?
3. Are you accountable to someone else such as a close friend and fellow Christian?
4. Do others see you as responsible and accountable for your actions?
5. Do they know that when you make a mistake that you will own up to it?

7

THEY PAY ATTENTION TO DETAILS

Spec Ops soldiers know that the devil is in the details. One missed observation can get a whole unit of men killed. One misstep means their buddies aren't coming home. They have a meticulous, almost obsessive attention to detail. They notice and pay attention to everything from the tonality used in a conversation to the number of exits in a restaurant (Quora).

The Old Testament talks about the building of the temple in exquisite detail, much more than I have room for here. It covers everything—from the height of the door posts, to the clothes of the priests, to their breastplates, curtains, lampstands, and even the dishes.

God is a very detailed God. He is interested in all the details in your life, from big things to small things. The problem is, we sometimes withhold some of the details to God. Maybe you have something that is important to you, but not a very big deal in the grand scheme of things. And so we may not pray about it like we should, thinking this isn't big enough to bother Him with it. Well, the book of James says that, "*We have not because we ask not.*" When God made you, He took into account every detail possible that makes you who you are today. Now be careful with that last statement. Some people will say, "Well, I am the way I am because that's how God made me" to account for their shortcomings, their personality, behavior, or habits. I'm pretty sure that excuse won't bode well with God when you stand before Him.

One Sunday at church, I noticed a police officer come into the sanctuary during the sermon and start looking under seats. I told my wife that something was up, although we didn't know what. Turns out, a man came into the church at the west lobby wearing a backpack. A lady noticed that it seemed kind of bulky and there was something sticking out of it, but she couldn't tell what it was. She was suspicious so she called church security who met him near the entrance to the sanctuary. When they asked to see his backpack, he got nervous and made a run for the sanctuary doors. Security was able to tackle him before he made entrance. They found one or two guns in the backpack. Because of the woman who paid attention to detail, a potential active shooter event was stopped before it happened.

How are you when it comes to others about detail? Are we listening to details when others talk that may tell us their hurting, or are we just trying to find a way to politely end the conversation? What about when you confess your sins to God? Are you being detailed about those sins in an attempt to come clean and get forgiveness? Or are we just asking for a blanket of forgiveness for all of them? The reason I ask is because calling those sins out by name is humbling. And the Lord likes humbleness. In turn, are you detailed in your prayers about requests? Or like confessing, are we asking for a blanket of blessings in all areas of our lives? When my wife and I pray for each other, we pray specifically for each body part. Sounds kind of silly without hearing it, but it is very detailed in order to cover each from head to toe in prayer.

Columbine

The event of April 20, 1999 was the most tragic case of school violence up to then that ever occurred in the US. Here is what happened according to CNN.com.

> **January 1998**—Dylan Klebold and Eric Harris
> are arrested after stealing items from a van. After
> pleading guilty, they are sent to a juvenile diver-
> sion program.

March 1998—Randy and Judy Brown, parents of student Brooks Brown, file a report with the sheriff's office stating that Harris had threatened to kill Brooks and had written on the internet that he would like to kill people.

April 20, 1999—At approximately 11:19 a.m., two students, Klebold, 17, and Harris, 18, carrying guns and bombs, open fire inside Columbine High School, killing 13 and wounding 23 others before killing themselves.

(Retrieved from: https://www.cnn.com/2013/09/18/us/columbine-high-school-shootings-fast-facts/index.html)

The shooters also had several homemade bombs that failed to go off. The father of Harris was a retired Air Force test pilot and, according to the article, was a strict disciplinarian. Also mentioned was the fact that Mr. Harris knew that his son was troubled and documented it in his journal, but did nothing beyond that. When authorities searched the house, they found bomb-making material under the bed that neither parent knew anything about.

The whole point of this story is that there was a failure by the parents to pick up on the finer details that if discovered, could have saved thirteen lives. How can you not know about explosives in your own home? I told both of my kids long ago that there is no such thing as privacy in my house. I will go through their room, drawers, and cars periodically as I see fit in order to keep on top of things. If they were hiding anything from me, it wouldn't be in my house. If you think that's overbearing, I don't care. Thankfully I never found anything of concern. Look, I wasn't being an authoritarian, I was being a dad. They always know they can talk to me about anything. Sure, I'm noisy when it comes to their plans and their friends. But I have always been, and will always be, engaged and involved in their lives. Attention to details, ladies and gentlemen. It will go a long way in taking your faith to the next level. And it may even save lives.

Takeaways

1. Are you paying attention to what's going on your families lives?
2. Do you know the names of your kids' friends and know them well?
3. Do you look through their belongings from time to time?
4. Are you attentive to when your wife seems distant?
5. Do you track the kids' phones to know where they are?
6. Do you go through their phones and look at texts they have sent or received?
7. Have you browsed their computer history to know what they have been looking at?

8

They Push Their Comfort Zone and Expand Their Capacity

Special Forces Operators are nothing if not overachievers, and this doesn't end when they leave the teams. When they return to civilian life, they almost always find a new way to expand their comfort zone and push their capacity to the next level. Whether this is through business, family, or hobbies, they always find ways to get more out of themselves and become better than they were the day before (Quora).

God doesn't care about your comfort zone. Comfort breeds passivity, passivity leads to laziness, and laziness stumps growth. Ecclesiastes 9:10 says, "*Whatever your hands find to do, do it with all your might.*" Moses wasn't comfortable when he was told by God to go to Pharaoh. In fact, he came up with a bunch of reasons why he wasn't the guy. But he was obedient. And because of his obedience, God did extraordinary things with and through him.

Embrace the Suck

When is the last time you got out of your comfort zone? How did that make you feel? You see, the military has a saying that goes "Be Comfortable Being Uncomfortable." The SEALs' motto is "The Only Easy Day Was Yesterday." The more comfortable you can become in uncomfortable situations, the more of an asset you are. A good way to do this is not look at the whole picture or task at once; rather, just focus on what's in front of you at that moment. Here's an example. I heard a story about a guy who was going through BUD/s to be a SEAL. The whole group was told they were going on a two-mile run down the beach and back. But when they got to the end of the two miles, the instructor yelled, "Sorry, ladies, it looks like we're going to be doing ten miles today instead of two." One guy was so disheartened, he rung out, eliminating him from training. He was so focused on the two miles that when two became ten, he couldn't mentally adapt and psyched himself out. They tell guys at BUD/s, only look at the next evolution. That's where the focus should be. As I mentioned earlier, that's how I got up the mountain in Colorado. Ten steps at a time.

A guy in my life group class is a perfect example of getting out of his comfort zone and expanding his capacity. His name is Terry, and he was once terrified of praying aloud with people, and witnessing to others. I mean, scared to almost the point of physically shaking. One Sunday night, our church had about a thousand people show up and go on an evangelizing mission, a short mission lasting only a couple of hours. We broke up into groups and were provided a map of the neighborhoods to hit. Terry and I were in the same group. The first house we came to, a family, sitting under the carport, had just celebrated someone's birthday. Terry saw the balloons tied to the mailbox and made his way to the carport. He asked whose birthday it was and said we had a gift for them (a gift bag provided by the church to hand out). I stood back and watched in awe as he talked to those people like they were his family. He was so relaxed and easygoing that it made them all feel like they had known each other for years. And to listen to him pray now was like listening to the Holy Spirit himself. He conquered his fears, he stepped out of his comfort zone, and because of it, God is using him in a remarkable way, and his faith has become so much stronger. I love this guy.

Face it, if you don't get out of your comfort zone and expand your capabilities, you're not going to be much use to God. Do you honestly think these missionaries who give up everything they know and uproot their families to go to some war-torn nation or Islamic nation or communist nation to share the gospel aren't somewhat afraid? How long do you think they're there before they start second-guessing their decision? But they do it out of obedience and love for the Savior.

So where do you start? Well, start pushing yourself physically when you exercise. We talked about this earlier so I won't rehash it, but do something to push yourself a little farther than you think you can go. Safely please. Remember, the physical feeds the mental, which is connected to the spiritual. Then think of something that makes you uncomfortable. Maybe it's witnessing like Terry, so start where you work. It doesn't have to be a full faith outline, but begin to engage a conversation and then work God into it. Talk about a death you heard about on the news and that opens the door to ask if they know where they are going when they die. People who know me will tell you if I just meet you, and I have a little time, no matter where we are in a conversation, I will steer that conversation toward God. People are so worried about offending others, or being rejected should they bring up God that keep their mouths shut. Have you ever stopped to think it may be you that is the last person they see before their life ends? And what if they listen to you and receive Christ? How cool would that be? But you will never know until you get out there and do it.

Something else that may help you get comfortable is participating in a mission trip. Before you start thinking you don't have the money to go overseas somewhere, there is plenty of mission work to be done where you are. Volunteer for a project that your church is doing or, better yet, apart from your church where the only person you know is you. God will get you through whatever it is you do. You just have to pray and be attentive to His presence. It won't be long, and you will certainly start becoming more comfortable in uncomfortable situations. To me, this one principle has the ability to really take your faith to that next level more than any other. But you won't know unless you try. You won't regret it.

Takeaways.

1. Is there anything that makes you uncomfortable doing?
2. What is something you can do to take you out of your comfort zone?
3. Is there something that you would like to get better at that is uncomfortable now?
4. What are some things you can do to expand your capabilities?

9

THEY PURSUE THEIR GOALS WITH EXTREME VIOLENCE OF ACTION (BEING INTENTIONAL)

When Tier 1 operators commit to a goal, they are *committed* to that goal. They have a saying in the teams to act with "Extreme Violence of Action." They don't wait at the gate for the enemy to come to them; they take the fight to the enemy with extreme force. They move decisively and eliminate any obstacles in their way (Quora). I added being intentional.

So what does it mean to use extreme violence of action? In the military world, this would be deadly action in the most violent ways against our enemies. In the Christian sense, violence of action would be to act decisively and aggressively to any ploy Satan throws at us with the tools God has given us—all the tools we've talked about in the previous chapters. Are you starting to feel regret for past wrongs? Attack those thoughts quoting scripture. Going through a difficult time? Start praising the One who will see you through. Having problems with the kids or the wife? Get on your knees and pour your heart out to the Lord with fervency and boldness. When you feel Satan start to attack, you attack back with ferociousness.

This is how we apply this principle to our Christian lives. Notice in the above text how Spec Op guys approach things with intent. They take the fight to the enemy, they move decisively, and they eliminate any obstacles. They are not waiting to be asked to join in something that someone else initiated. I mentioned it earlier, but will elaborate more on it here. They are being intentional. We have to be intentional in our faith because we are not always going to want to be faithful in acting or responding as Christ would have us to.

I believe that this one principle should apply to all the other principles presented in this book. Let's review. Are you intentional in thinking about why you are a Christian? Do you now have a compelling answer as to why so it sparks those who aren't Christians to think about why they are not and the consequences that come with not being saved?

Are you intentional about how you're training your body, mind, and spirit for this war on Christianity, pushing and challenging yourself in the process?

Are you intentional about getting an early start to the day and setting and achieving goals?

Are you being intentional about discovering your purpose that God has for you, and will you pursue that purpose?

What about being intentional in cultivating strong bonds? Will you pursue that accountability relationship with one or more men or women and pray for them regularly?

Are you being intentional about taking ownership of your responsibilities and leading your family well?

Are you intentional about paying close attention to the details in the lives of your family members and others?

And are or will you be intentional about getting out of your comfort zone and expanding your capacity and influence? I hope you can see that this principle is a good fit for all the other principles we've talked about.

Why is this so important? As mentioned moments ago, we are not always going to want to act or respond like we should. When you roll out of bed in the morning, is your attitude like, "Well, crap, another day of going to work at this stupid job," or is it more like, "Thank you, Lord, for another day that I can be a blessing to someone." Can you see the difference? It's all about attitude. And let's face it, somedays we just don't feel like being a blessing. In fact, some days we could care less. But being intentional allows us to recognize this and then make that conscious effort to fight through it. This is where we make up our mind that no matter how we may feel at that moment, we intentionally decide that we are going to be a blessing to someone. Being intentional helps us to put others before self. And to my recollection, isn't that what Jesus tells us to do? The disciples were all intentional in sharing the gospel in places that didn't show them much favor. And what did they get for it? Beaten, whipped, flogged, arrested, spit on, abused, shunned, and eventually killed. But did that stop them? Nope! (Well, except for the death part, but the other stuff didn't.) Do you think they felt like getting beaten? No. They knew it was coming, but they saw the bigger picture. They knew that they were going to be uncomfortable when the consequences of preaching about Jesus came their way, but that didn't matter. They knew too much was at stake. They were obedient even to the point of death.

Matthew 6:33 says, "*Seek first the kingdom of God and His righteousness, and all these things will be given to you as well.*" Being intentional starts with true commitment to God and expanding His kingdom. Are we seeking His ways first with no regard for our own? Let's look at what true commitment is.

Burn the Ships

Burn The Ship was born from an idea that originated in 1519. That year, Hernán Cortés set sail to Veracruz, Mexico with his crew. Upon arrival, Cortés' men became weary and scared, with hopes of turning back home to their old life.

As legend has it, Cortez had the men burn their ships, leaving no option but to press on! Their ability to retreat to their previous way of life was gone; their safety net had been removed.

The burning of those ships represented much more than a separation from old ways. The same fire that set the ships ablaze also allowed

Cortés men to complete their mission and be a part of something greater than themselves.

Burning our ships means there is no turning back to old habits and ways. In this world we wrestle with all kinds of different physical, mental, emotional, and spiritual battles. To allow great change in our lives, we must find the root of those struggles—our own ships that can be so tempting to sail back on—and burn them. (Retrieved from https://www.weburntheship. com/the-story)

Now that's true commitment. Are there any ships in your life you need to burn in order to grow closer to God? Is there anything hampering your relationship with Him? Maybe you're a little too flirtatious with a coworker even though you're married. Or maybe you're talking to an old flame on Facebook when you shouldn't be. Maybe you enjoy alcohol a little too much. Is there anything on the internet that comes across your screen from time to time that shouldn't? Are you treating your wife or husband the way you should? Are you praying for him or her like you should? There are a number of things that will keep you from growing in the Lord unless you give it to Him. I used to cuss like a sailor. Every other word out of my mouth seemed to be profane. And then I got saved. Did it stop? It slowed down. But then the Lord really convicted me of my colorful use of language. Now some of you are probably saying to yourself, "Come on, dude, it's just words." Yeah well, the Bible does say not to use filthy language. It tells us no coarse (dirty or inappropriate) joking as well. But what opened my eyes was the verse that says we will have to answer to Him for every word spoken (Matt. 12:36), which for me means God better bring a comfortable chair 'cause we're going to be there a while.

Look, we are told to be ambassadors for Christ. When we cuss, people can't see Christ in us. Plain and simple. The fact that the Bible says it is good enough for me. These are just some of the things that will stunt your growth. Take it to the Lord, lay it at the cross, and leave it there. When we accept salvation, we are to die to ourselves. No sin is so small that God will overlook it. This could be considered as paying attention to detail liked we talked about in an earlier chapter. Be faithful with the little things and He will make you faithful with much!

Keep this in mind. When we are intentional in these areas regarding our faith, this is pursuing our goals with extreme violence of action, (VOA). But this violence of action is not directed at man, but at the devil himself! We are taking control of our lives and giving Satan none of it! We will violently protect and take action against the one who wants to cause us and our family harm by giving Christ control of every area of our lives.

Takeaways

1. What in your life do you need to be more intentional about?
2. Is there anything in your life that you need to attack with extreme VOA that may be preventing you from being fully committed to the Lord?
3. Are you committed to fixing the little things that don't seem like a big deal so you can better your relationship with the Lord? A bunch of little things will become a big thing.

10

SPECIAL FORCES OPERATORS REFUSE TO QUIT

These guys just don't quit. For SEALs, BUD/s last six months and has an 80 percent attrition rate. This means that for every one hundred men who attempt to become SEALs, only 20 percent pass the first phase of training. Most experts estimate that only two out of every one hundred men who attempt SEAL training will actually earn their tridents. Failure is not an option for them. They'd rather die than give up. That is why they win, because they do not give up (Quora).

If you put one warrior against ten bad guys, his mind-set will be to fight to the death. He won't complain about it, and he won't fret about it. He is going to think, "Well, I may die, but let's see how many of these guys I can take out first." He is going to fight like he is the third monkey on the ramp to Noah's ark, and brother, it's starting to rain! That is the mind-set of a warrior.

We live in a time where if anything gets remotely difficult in life, people just give up. Don't believe me, just look at the divorce rates in this country. You know it's bad when the number of married couples getting divorced outnumber the couples who stay married. I had heard at one time that the divorce rate in the church was almost 50 percent, though I can't back that up with sources. Divorce is so common now that the government has come up with no-fault divorce. It streamlines the process so you can be single again in a shorter amount of time. I went to a wedding once, and they had ads for divorce lawyers on the back of the invitations. Okay, I'm kidding with that one. But so much for "'til death do us part." A coworker of mine told me once that they even have yellow cards in the military now. If you're going through boot camp and need a longer rest, or can't take the drill sergeant screaming at you anymore, just pull the card and go sit quietly.

Galatians 6:9 says, "*And let us not grow weary of doing good, for in due season we will reap, if we do not give up.*" Look, I get it. As I said at the start of this book, the Christian life is hard. But it's worth it! It is up to us to stay strong and to keep trudging on. Our nation, our freedom to worship openly, and most importantly, our families depend on it. Where would we be today if Jesus decided, "Hey, this is too hard. I'm tired of taking a beating for other people. I'm done with this crap." You know where we would be, or soon be. In the bowels of hell! But He didn't quit. He knew that too much was on the line. So much was at stake. And to think even though we spit in His face, turn our backs on Him, and shake our fist in His face, saying "Not Your will, but mine be done," He still endured the cross. He saw it through to the end.

When are we going to stop quitting? Don't like your job? Just quit. Marriage not working out? Quit. After all, the grass is greener on the other side, right? *Wrong!* The grass is greener where you water it. Having problems with the kids? Just stay at work longer. You could use the extra money. Don't like the music in church? Find another church to go to. Or just stay home and watch it on television.

I have always told my kids as they grew up to take the hard road. It's much more satisfying when you get to the end. Choose what's hard because you will be better for it. Some people quit because they are afraid of failing. But if looked at with the right perspective, they would realize that failure is just another rung on the ladder to success. Failure spurs growth, if you don't quit. The household product 409 is named that because it took them that many times to get it right. No joke. Same with WD-40. Take a weight lifter. His muscles grow because of the resistance of the weights. And as the muscles grow, he becomes stronger. He pushes his muscles to the point of failure. Then as he sleeps, the muscles break down, and as a result, he gets bigger. Resistance causes growth. If he quit when the weights got hard to lift, he wouldn't see any growth.

I was praying for a year for a business deal to come through. I run a business on my off days from the fire department. Oh, how I prayed specifically for this deal to happen. Finally, after a year of consistent prayer, I got an answer from the other players involved. It was a "thank you but no." I didn't even consider quitting. I accepted it as an answer to prayer even though it wasn't the answer I was praying for. What are you going to do when God tells you no? Are you just going to throw in the towel and call it quits? I hope not. It would be to your detriment. One of the biggest regrets you will ever have is quitting. Can you learn from it? Oh sure. Still sucks, though. You already know this, but I will say it anyway. It takes a bigger person to follow something through to the end than it does to quit. Quitters never win, and winners never quit. Both of my kids played sports all through their childhood. My daughter was so upset after practice one day she wanted to quit. I told her she could quit when the season was over, but not before. If you commit to something, you see it through.

As far as the Christian life goes, there are a lot of quitters. They get mad at God when something bad happens or when someone from the church has wronged them. I'm watching a young lady now who was so involved in church for years and has godly parents, just turn her back on everything having to do with God. And what does she do? Like so many others, she blames the church. FYI, there is no perfect church. Church is a hospital for sinners. If you're looking for examples to inspire you, look no further than the ones I gave you earlier in the book. Remember the couple that lost all six kids in one horrific accident? The parents' response is pretty inspiring. How about Job? Remember his story? Satan took his livestock, his home, and worst of all, his children—all of them. And Job stayed faithful to the end. Even after his own wife and three friends basically told him to give up and quit on God. But he didn't. And because of that, God blessed him with double what he had before, including his children.

These ten principles are just one resource out of many to help your faith grow. It's past time to take your relationship with Him to the next level, to know God on a deeper level. Write them down, share them with others, be intentional with each principle, and watch your faith go to new heights. You will be blessed and, in turn, be better equipped to be a blessing to others.

Takeaways

1. Share with others anything that you quit and why.
2. Have you ever wanted to quit but pushed through to complete it anyway? How did you feel afterward?
3. What made you want to keep going?
4. How did not quitting shape you into the person you are today?

This book is not only about developing a deeper relationship with God but strengthening your mind-set as well. Do you remember the verse I used to open this book?

> Be transformed by the renewing of your mind.
> (Rom. 12:2)

Being a Christian is like anything else in life. You have to train your mind for it. It is a mind-set! You don't have to be an alpha male or female in order to live the Christian life, but you don't have to be so passive that the world runs you over either. We are only empowered when we choose to move forward. Listen to this and write it down if you can't remember it.

Well-known pastor and author John Hagee said, "You're never going to outgrow warfare. You simply must learn to fight." He said, "I've heard people say, 'oh, woe is me, when is it going to get easier?' When you *die*! Warfare is a normal New Testament Christian posture. Get used to it!"

Start preparing your mind for battle on a daily basis. Prepare yourself physically, mentally, emotionally, and spiritually. We live in a day of snowflakes and safe spaces. No one likes to think about losing a loved one to death, but it is going to happen. A study in the *New England Journal of Medicine* showed that a hundred out of one hundred people die (insert laughter). I made a call one night where a ninety-seven-year-old man was in cardiac arrest. He was eaten up with cancer and sent home to die. When I arrived, the family did not have a do-not-resuscitate form. I asked them what they wanted to do. They told me they wanted us to do everything we could to save him.

Did I mention he was ninety-seven years old! They did not prepare themselves for the inevitable.

Something that will help you do this is to get rid of the distractions. Can you see where I'm going with this? Put down the cell phone. We have become a nation of zombies. I walked into a restaurant once and saw a large party of about ten people sitting around a table. Nine were looking at their phone. It baffles me as to how people think they are so important now that they can't miss anything that comes across their phone. Put it down and go outside. Take a walk in nature, and if you want to take a picture, take a camera with you. Remember those? Technology has gotten so good with cameras that the Japanese has invented a camera with a shutter speed so fast that you can actually capture a woman with her mouth closed (Just kidding, ladies).

Putting all or just some of these principles into practice is showing God that you are willing to go above and beyond that of the everyday Christian. And in doing so, He will show you a part of Him that you've never seen or experienced before. And that is what I want out of my walk with the Lord—to know Him better and to have a deeper experience with Him than I have ever experienced before. After all, He should have written me off long ago. But He didn't. And I am so grateful that He never gave up on me.

So what do you do now? Well if you are a Christian, then just start putting these principles into action. Pray for our country, as we badly need it. Be a blessing to someone every day, even if it's no more than paying a compliment to a stranger and bringing a smile to their face.

And maybe on the off chance you're not a Christian, and you just picked up this book by accident, then there is a lot you can do. The Bible says that "For God so loved the world (you), that he gave his only begotten son (Jesus), that who-so-ever (you) believes in Him (Jesus), shall not perish, but have ever-lasting life." If you want to know the Lord Jesus on a personal level, if you are tired of going through life's difficulties alone, just pray this simple prayer.

Say, "Lord Jesus, I know I'm a sinner. And I know I need a savior. Lord, forgive me of all my sins, past, present, and future. Come into my heart, cleanse me in your blood, and save me, Lord Jesus. I make you my Lord and Savior. Thank you for saving me. Help me to trust in you and live for you every day. I love you, Jesus. Help that love grow more and more every day. In the name of Jesus, I pray, amen!"

If you prayed that prayer, welcome to the family of God. You are a child of the One True King! Start reading His Word daily and spend time in prayer and thanksgiving to Him every day. Find a Bible-believing church and let them know you are a new creature in Christ. Start reading the book of John in the New Testament and find fellowship with other Christians.

Maybe you are already saved and have turned away, and you feel the Lord calling you back. Just pray this: "Lord Jesus, I'm sorry for my rebellion against You. Forgive me where I have failed You. Lord, create in me a new heart and fill me with Your Holy Spirit. Help me to live for you every day of my life. Thank You for never giving up on me. Jesus, I love You, and I pray this in Christ's name, amen!"

If you are someone who enjoyed this book or prayed to receive Christ or renew your relationship with him, please let me know. I can be reached at gary.panzer@gmail.com. I would love to celebrate with you. Please see the bonus section on mental toughness starting on the next page.

Thank you for reading!

Life is not a journey to the grave with the intention of arriving safely with a pretty and preserved body; but rather to skid in broadside, thoroughly used up, totally worn out and loudly proclaiming "Wow! What a ride!"
—*Fearless: The Adam Brown Story*

Bonus

Need a little help with mental toughness? I have you covered. Meet David Goggins. He is all over the internet. I highly recommend you pull up an interview with him on YouTube, as copyrights prevent me from using his picture.

David Goggins is the toughest man alive.

There's no doubt about it. Goggins is the only member of the US Armed Forces to complete SEAL training, US Army Ranger School, and Air Force Tactical Air Controller training.

Any of those accomplishments alone would have been impressive, but that's not all.

He's also the current Guinness record holder for the most number of pull-ups done in twenty-four hours. Alongside that record are multiple first-place finishes at the most brutal ultra-endurance events, which attracts the toughest competitors from around the world.

How does someone consistently push himself to his physical and mental limits all the time?

Let's find out.

Lesson 1: Purpose trumps motivation.

David Goggins doesn't believe in motivation. In his own words, "Motivation is crap. Motivation comes and goes."

Purpose, on the other hand, is something that Goggins can get behind.

After some of his fellow SEALs were killed in a military operation, Goggins signed up for the San Diego One Day, where he needed to run a hundred miles to qualify for future ultramarathons. His intention was to raise money for the Special Operations Warrior Foundation.

The problem?

Goggins hadn't put on running shoes at all in the past year. He was not a runner. Weighing anywhere from 240–270 pounds, he was more into powerlifting than anything else. Armed with a folding chair and a bag of crackers, Goggins entered the race.

He would pay dearly for his lack of preparation.

Through sheer force of will, Goggins made it to the seventy-mile mark. But the process had been brutal.

He had broken all the metatarsal bones in his feet. There were stress fractures, shin splints, and muscles tearing. He was peeing blood down his leg because he couldn't make it to a toilet twenty feet from him.

Even after finishing Navy SEAL and Ranger school training, the hundred-mile race was the toughest challenge Goggins had faced yet. He was on the brink of death, but he didn't quit. He went on slowly to finish the race, finishing the one hundred miles well within the allocated twenty-four hours.

How did he do it? Was it the mental strength that came from his cause? It would seem that way, but that's not what really happened:

"Everyone asks me, were you thinking about the guys that died at that time? I'm not gonna lie; I wasn't. This became a personal thing, this became me against this race; me against the kids that called me ni**er; me against me. It just became something I took so violently personal."

Pain obliterates our ability to think and function. But David Goggins was fueled by a purpose greater than himself, something more compelling than that pain.

It turns out that you can still keep going if you have such a purpose.

Lesson 2: Deconstruct things.

So how exactly did Goggins power through the remaining thirty miles?

"I broke this thing down into small pieces. I said I got to get nutrition; I got to be able to stand up before I can go through the 30 miles [...] I taped up my ankles, and then my feet, and that's how I got through that race."

It's an experience the SEAL would likely never forget.

This lesson of mental deconstruction has its roots in a process that all Navy SEALs must go through—hell week. It's the toughest period of SEAL training; trainees are put through 125 hours of continuous training, and typically get only two hours of sleep during that period. They're constantly cold, wet, and miserable.

The idea is to drain the trainees physically and mentally and then see what sort of decisions they make. Instructors do their best to make trainees ring the bell, which is used to announce that they're quitting. Nobody holds back here.

David Goggins went through three hell weeks—all in a span of a year.

Rolled over from his previous two classes first due to illness and then to injury, he was given one last chance to complete SEAL training. Goggins did just that, focusing on one challenge at a time. He would eventually graduate in this final attempt.

No obstacle is insurmountable. We find that there's always step that's actionable. Add up the small bits, and we would've accomplished something we never thought possible.

One step at a time is how hundred-mile marathons get completed.

Lesson 3: Remember the 40 percent rule.

Unbeknownst to Goggins, Jesse Itzler was participating in the same San Diego One Day race as well. The only difference was that he had participated with a six-man relay team.

Intrigued by how Goggins had manically completed the race despite his brutal injuries, Itzler invited the SEAL to live with him for a month. He wanted to learn more about the man that had finished a race despite being so ill-prepared. Goggins agreed with one condition: Itzler would do anything he said, no matter what.

On the first day, Itzler was made to do a hundred pull-ups.

Itzler did eight on his first set, then six, and then fewer still. His arms were aching, but Goggins wouldn't relent. He stood and watched as Itzler struggled, doing one pull-up at a time.

Itzler would finish his repetitions. In his book *Living with a SEAL*, Itzler said,

He [Goggins] showed me, proved to me right there that there was so much more, we're all capable of so much more than we think we are. [...] He would say that when your mind is telling you you're done, you're really only 40 percent done.

Research suggests that statement—the 40 percent rule—has some truth. We are often physically more capable than we perceive ourselves to be. For instance, researchers found that subjects who were given a placebo but told it was caffeine were able to lift significantly more weight than those who were really given caffeine.

There's a reserve tank within us that we never really tap into. Only by pushing ourselves to our limits—and then breaking them—can we reach our full potential.

Lesson 4: Mental visualization.

David Goggins believes that he's the toughest man on the planet. He thinks that he can complete virtually any task set before him.

He probably can. But the point is that you have to see yourself accomplishing something before it really happens. The mind has to conceive it before the body can achieve it.

The question he asks himself in times of struggle contains only two simple words: what if?

When he first walked into the Navy SEAL recruiter's office, Goggins was told that there were only thirty-five African-Americans in the past seventy years who had made it through. Goggins asked himself, "What if I could be the 36th?"

These days, he asks himself the same question whenever he's struggling through a run. It's this question that helps him get through when his body and mind are broken and begging for him to stop.

Seeing himself succeed and do the impossible gives him the shivers. That drives him to attack every day and challenge with a vengeance.

Lesson 5: Use your cookie jar.

Goggins has a secret weapon that he calls upon when he's about to break.

Like many others, he has a cookie jar that he reaches into for the occasional treat. But this jar doesn't contain any of the things you might typically find; there are no Oreos or Chips Ahoy cookies in there.

Instead, it contains every setback he has overcome. He'll remember that he's a Navy SEAL who's completed hell week three times. He'll remind himself that he's been through this pain before—and survived. The obstacle in front of him is nothing compared to what he has faced.

"Even the toughest man, in times of suffering, we forget how tough we really are"

Goggins never dwells on his accomplishments. The only time he revisits them is when he needs extra fuel for a push he's making. He allows himself to reach into his cookie jar only when there's a need. It's never a treat.

In contrast, I often find myself admiring a piece of work I've done that I'm particularly pleased with. Like many others who do this, it's ego that's being stroked here.

We would accomplish so much more if we spent our time doing the work and then occasionally looking back at how far we've come. The cookie jar should be used for fuel and not a distraction.

Lesson 6: Be willing to suffer

You wouldn't know it, but Goggins hates running.

He hates it with a passion. Growing up, Goggins has always been on the larger side. He loved powerlifting and had the physique to show for it. But in the world of ultra, such a large frame is virtually unheard of. It was just inefficient to move that much weight over such long distances.

Goggins knew he was going to suffer—that was precisely his plan. That was the only way he was going to raise enough funds for the Special Operations Warrior Foundation.

"People respond to pain. If I go out and wash cars for $10, who gives a damn? People want to see you throw up, cry and go through tremendous suffering."

But for David Goggins, suffering is not just about raising funds. As he says, "Suffering is the true test of life."

Goggins isn't training just for a race. He's training for the tragedies that inevitably strike each and every one of us. He does this so he doesn't fall apart if he gets the 2:00 a.m. call from the hospital informing him that his mother has passed away.

In other words, David Goggins is the modern-day stoic. But unlike the ancient philosophers who advised that we should periodically embrace suffering, Goggins has actually made suffering a habit.

Strengthen your mind and your resolve by voluntarily putting yourself through situations in which you struggle. Callus your mind the same way you do your hands. Take the path of most resistance every day of your life.

That's how David Goggins has become the toughest man alive. And according to him, the happiest as well: "Having lived the life I've lived, and having seen the other side, not being afraid to attack what was in front of me, has made me happy."

Physical Limitations

Here comes the kicker.

Up until 2010, David Goggins had been living with an undetected congenital heart defect, which essentially left him with a hole in his heart.

The condition leaves his heart functioning only at 75 percent capacity and typically prevents people from engaging in activities such as scuba diving or anything at high altitude.

And yet David Goggins has led an exemplary military career, with multiple athletic achievements in his name.

It's absurd what he's been able to do despite the numerous disadvantages he was saddled with.

Perhaps some of us are wired differently. Maybe he isn't human at all.

Or maybe, we just need to leave our excuses at the door.

Developing mental toughness is as brutal as it sounds, so I'll give it to you straight: *stop caring what others think.*

That is 99 percent of it, right there.

Most people live their entire lives pleasing others, not wanting to look silly because of what they love to do, afraid of failing because it will look bad, not taking chances in something they want, or not even getting assistance with their problems because they feel it looks weak.

Screw that.

Developing mental toughness asks you to be authentic, no matter what that looks like, by gradually exposing yourself to more and more challenging situations and circumstances.

Oftentimes, you will hear so-called experts and gurus telling you to just

- toughen up,
- quit being a little b——h,
- man up, or
- do it!

And all sorts of other well-intentioned but generally ineffective advice.

The truth of the matter is this: if you want to become mentally tougher, you need to do so gradually and with a comprehensive plan.

You won't go from being a slob to a Navy SEAL overnight, and that's okay.

Here are five ways you can increase your mental toughness over time to become the strongest and most mentally resilient person you know.

1. Embrace the cold (shower).

    One of the simplest but most effective ways to increase your mental toughness is the cold shower.

    While the physical health benefits of cold showers have been largely over blown, the mental effects have not.

    Cold showers suck. There's nothing fun about them. And it takes tons of mental strength to intentionally subject yourself to the icy blasts. Start slow and work your way up. For the first week, take a shower as normal and then turn the water all the way cold for the last thirty seconds. For the second week, increase it to sixty seconds, then two minutes, three minutes, four minutes, and so on until you can take a ten-minute cold shower with ease.

There's something magical about subjecting yourself to this kind of physical torture that builds strength and mental resilience in a way few things can.

Give this a go for thirty days, and I promise you will feel the effects.

2.   Train hard and give it all you've got.

The second way that you can build mental toughness is by building physical toughness through resistance training and intense cardio.

Since everyone is starting at a different point of physical strength, I recommend that you start out small.

Spend one week setting benchmarks for your

- one-mile run time,
- bench press, deadlift, squat, and overhead press max,
- push-up, pull-up, and sit-up max.

And then slowly push yourself to go harder than you've gone before.

For example, if you can only do twenty-five push-ups this week, set a goal to do thirty push-ups next week.

Grind it out. Push yourself. Keep going until you have nothing left in the tank. You might be surprised at how much stronger your body is than you imagined.

Often times, we are stronger physically than we are mentally, and we can actually do more than we ever thought if we can break through our mental barriers.

Make a habit of setting and crushing goals in the gym, and I promise the mental toughness you cultivate will spread to every other area of your life.

3. Use thirty-day challenges to accelerate your toughness and personal growth.

We all have vices. We all have things that we wish we could do but seem unable to make stick. More often than not, the reason that we struggle with these things is that we try and bite off too much in the beginning.

For example, we decide that we are going to

- quit smoking forever,
- never drink alcohol again, or
- give up video games.

And the list goes on.

Most of us try to completely and permanently eradicate our bad habits. And it gets so intimidating that we quickly fail and fall right back into our old ways. So I'd like to propose a different approach.

Instead of giving something up or taking up a new activity like meditation or exercise forever, start small

Commit to thirty days of following a habit or giving up a habit.

Tough it out for those thirty days and then decide whether or not you want to keep the new habit in place.

You'll find that by breaking down difficult tasks into bite-sized chunks, you can quickly build mental toughness and become a success machine.

4.   Use positive self-talk to keep yourself going.

We all talk to ourselves whether you realize it or not. In any given moment, there are a dozen conversations going on in your head telling you who to be and how you should feel. The problem is that most of us aren't aware of these conversations. And we sure as heck aren't consciously controlling them.

If you want to build rock-solid mental toughness, then you need to talk to yourself like a mentally tough person would.

Start using affirmations like

- I've got this,
- No pain, no gain,
- Just push through,
- C'mon, just one more, and other similar phrases.

By improving your self-talk and creating an empowering conversation in your head, you will quickly improve your mental toughness and ability to handle challenges.

5.   Face your fears slowly.

The final way that you can build mental toughness and become more resilient is by gradually exposing yourself to your fears and phobias and proving that you are stronger than your fears.

We're all scared of something.

Some of us fear rejection; some of us fear change, physical hardship, or loss of love.

And the best way to overcome these fears is to expose yourself to them.

If you want to build your mental toughness, then you must eradicate your fears overtime by gradually exposing yourself to them.

For example, if you are afraid of rejection, take a part-time sales job cold calling prospects and watch as your fear vanishes.

If you are afraid of losing everything you've built in your life, take three to four days and literally be homeless for a weekend. Spend less than $10 a day and sleep under the stars.

You will quickly find yourself asking, "Is this what I really feared?"

The more you can expose yourself to your biggest fears, the more mentally tough you will be.

Start small and work your way up.

I promise, it will have a profound impact on your life and success.

(Retrieved from: https://constantrenewel.com/david-goggins)

REFERENCES

Evans, Tony. *Kingdom Man*. Carol Stream, Ill.: Tyndale House Publishers, 2012.

Myers, C. Forbes.com. "The 40% Rule: The Simple Secret to Success." Retrieved from https://www.forbes.com/sites/chrismyers/2017/10/06/the-40-rule-the-simple-secret-to-success/#14ec-3305cdd8, 2017.

Quora.com.

Eric Brand, printed with permission.

Wallace Lock, printed with permission.

Commercial Appeal, (April 20, 2019). Religion in America Today. Commercialappeal.com.

Ruiz, R. Forbes.com. https://www.forbes.com/2007/11/14/health-obesity-cities-forbeslife-cx_rr_1114obese.html#8f91203750f5, 2012.

James Lindsey, printed with permission.

CNN Library, CNN. "Columbine High School Shootings Fast Facts." Retrieved from https://www.cnn.com/2013/09/18/us/columbine-high-school-shootings-fast-facts/index.html, 2017.

Burn the Ships, (n.d.). Retrieved from https://www.weburntheship.com/the-story.

Lion of Judah, (n.d.). YouTube. [Video]. John Hagee. Retrieved from https://www.youtube.com/watch?v=bRrjNnKPLpk&list=PLoM-9CL4f9khfjJE23kgzp_K0Fnf45ZyxH&index=3&t=0s.

Blehm, E. *Fearless: The Undaunted Courage and Ultimate Sacrifice of Navy SEAL Team SIX Operator Adam Brown*. Published by WaterBrook Press 12265 Oracle Boulevard, Suite 200 Colorado Springs, CO 80921, 2012.

David Goggins, (n.d.). Retrieved from: https://constantrenewel.com/david-goggins.